Yamma

Yamma

Poems by

Elizabeth Poreba

Cover design by Shay Culligan
Cover image by Giulia Bertelli on Unsplash
Author photo by John Poreba

ISBN: 978-1-63980-608-9

Kelsay Books
502 South 1040 East, A-119
American Fork, Utah 84003
Kelsaybooks.com

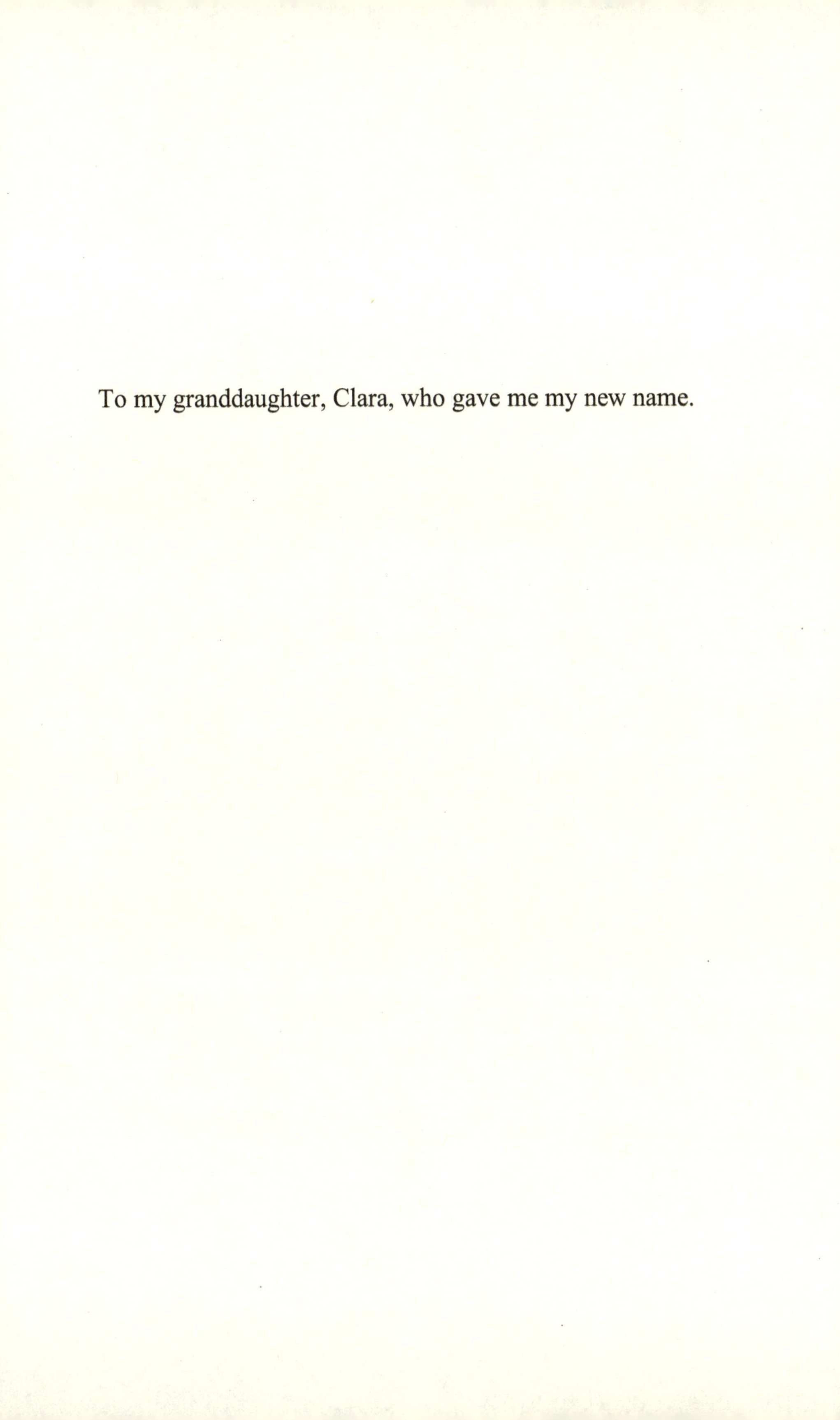

To my granddaughter, Clara, who gave me my new name.

Acknowledgment

Thank you to the following publication, in which a version of this poem previously appeared:

The Journal of Feminist Studies in Religion: "Accuracy"

Contents

A Joyful Mind Maketh Age Flourishing

Your Crazy Grandmother

Yamma After the Ferry Ride

We took the ride and then
I read the poem aloud to her with heart.

I read louder and kept looking up.

And you that shall cross from shore to shore years hence

I read with force,
I pointed to her for effect.

Let her remember me, the dotty grandmother.

The others that are to follow me, the ties between me and them

Let her remember her crazy grandmother.

Not About Yamma's Body

I look down and there it is, the obvious
topic, tacit

and usually quiet. We all have one.
Mine likes toast, sleep, clean sheets, sun.

It is not my topic here. Let's stay
eye to eye—but not the actual

eyes—not my topic—I want to be we two
gathered in brightness, minds meeting in air.

Keats took his living hand and held it out to you
unblemished, practically new,

but this one—thick knuckles, brown spots, skin too sheer
to cover the veins' slow work—not my topic here.

The Half-Baked Ideas I Live By

Flour water
yeast sugar
not enough
of one or
the other
or there's
something wrong
that's not
my fault.
Maybe I was
too hasty or
a problem
with the recipe.

Remember
that hard tack
our ancestors
in the faith
had to pack
as they decamped?
Got to go
with what
we've got.
Here's a knife
and butter.
Next time
maybe
better luck.

Looks like bread anyway.
Probably okay.

Yamma Imagines She Is a Museum and Her Granddaughter Is an Indifferent Tourist

I offer nothing spectacular—
a telephone dial, a typewriter—
even the script in which I scrawl
this request, hoping to pique,
your historical interest
in conditions peculiar
to settlers along New England rivers,
who dammed and built factories
in God-shadowed puzzlement and misery.

Thousands of dams! So much to hold back!

Your LA River cannot compete,
sliding along algaed concrete,
housed by the town as if on charity,
more run-off than tributary,
lacking volume enough to bear
any more than itself, leaving
denizens to chance—no depth—
no dark—no sustenance.

Spring Vacation

She came to visit in March, my unhappy mother,
younger than I am now, with a large suitcase
and a matching carry-on for medications.
The weather was like this, grey and damp.
"Never so cold in my life," she said
of my drafty house. The mold disturbed her allergies.
Once she helped me out in the yard where we,
at ease with acts of drudgery, heaped dead leaves
for the brisk brook to bear away.
                                        Mostly we stayed
inside, her by the wood stove, me prolonging
my paperwork, my daughter upstairs with her radio.
Days and days of not saying as she talked and talked
or watched the news while I cooked.
                                        It rained and then not.
Outside, in a wet disorder of flung branches
and last summer's cigarettes on thatched grass,
the lawn was revving up for a celebration:
some crocus, a few robins tuning, and a sky so blue
it felt too lavish for us, prodigal.

Alimentary

We're *thinking reeds,*
but who wants to think
about that tube,
core, conduit that
turns food to thought,
tears, music, and all
the hijinks and nonsense,
before returning it
back to substance?

Why do we reduce
the end to expletive
or baby talk when
this, in each of us
operating on its
own (more or less)
is marvelous?

Worms

There I am nursing grievances, washing the dishes,
calculating my steps, my pulse, my innermost thoughts,
writing checks, poems, petitions, buying wine by the box—

while humble, slimy, not discernibly dissatisfied,
and carbon negative, they are aerating,
feeding, defecating, through muck and drought—
contributing to the world's grain harvest as much as Russia.

This is how we sing as the species' ship goes down,
I read, lyrics about loss, loss, all for nought,
despair, *Ruin from the air—*

On the flyways, birds tack against the winds, old haunts dried up.
On highways, creatures dart and feint, everywhere fire,
or engorged rivers sluice excess over asphalt —

No use trying to resign from this ferocity,
tangled, alive, voracious,
unlovely as the worms that feed us.

Mishap

My Liquid Cover Up slipped off the shelf.
I wasn't looking as I readied myself
for the daily layer, its effect gone,
I know, by afternoon, but done
Not to frighten the horses,
as my mother used to say.

Anyway *Crash,* glass in shards and goo
beading on the sponge, forming
pellets in sink water and tanning the grout.

I'm out $20, and I'm glad, worth the price,
sign from heaven, too late for artifice—

Yamma Reads Iris Murdoch's Definition of Humility

In all humility, I can say
"A selfless respect for reality"
has guided my lifelong
low expectations,
though I do
go overboard
in pride
in moderation—
the excess of—
the didn't dos,
didn't say,
didn't love—
preferences
for the cut-rate way,
habits from birth,
family tradition
of low worth
and scarcity.
But there I go again
bragging about
my tendency,
not a big deal.
Overall, I just
got through,
a lucky girl.

Yamma Considers Youthful Energy

So young, yet they go about doing things,
making rockets, books, boats, grenades,
hieroglyphics, crucifixions, constructions
over chasms, cities on stilts,
younger than I am, and no hesitation,
a few instructions and off they go,
I Do, I Will, You Will—
malls and landing strips,
while the wind tears terrible howls
from off the fraught sea to bend the pines
above their deep-dug habitations—

So young and certain
as the planet keeps unmaking,
loss after loss, layers of *loess*—
matter made of mammoth-bone bits
and snail shells double-sorted
by wind and water—dust
geologically recent,
compared to humans ancient,
along the Rhine, all over Iowa,
color of the Yellow River,
succumbing softly to the plow
blowing where it will.

Knocking at the Gate

Yamma's Whiteness

"Fishbelly white," she complained.
(What was her name?) "Too fair," she said,
meaning the sun excised her skin
and left her pink.
                                        I was not too fair, but fair
enough, and serious in tanning: baby oil, iodine,
mostly the legs, long brown legs crucial
in the prevailing story of a beach, a pool,
sports on wide green fields.
                                                            I played
that role, concocting from my chaise
(aluminum, a small lawn) a girl
who fit the prevailing tale, the queen
pictured in the magazines.

Yamma Probes the Problem of Evil

It took me time to notice
that it existed, not only
in mild forms such as roadside trash
and family tiffs, but maniacally,
blatant, full of glee and
even a threat to my safety.

Shouldn't someone be doing
something about this? I asked
and was told that it was not
my personal discovery,
but part of the furniture,
the inherited armoire,
the leering portrait in the foyer.

Yeah, they'd say. *You know—*
Beezlebub, The Prince of Darkness?
with a smile for the childhood cartoons.
Then I knew who he was,
recalled my head on his chest,
the comfort of my vested interests.

Final Act

What's done cannot be undone

felt wrong. So much we did
we'd undo to do again.
The sun, bird song
and so on.The road
to town went up
then down.We thought
we could swim
in the same river
twice.We thought
our hum drum
would suffice.

Not on the first fire-
hazed day, or when
the river surged
over the highway,
but finally,
the messengers arrived.

They do not wait.
All day, all night, we hear
them *knocking at the gate.*

Yamma Wonders What Her Grandchildren Will Fear

Not the wolf at first   favored top predator
that old fear will be gone

though I suppose   time to come
as the trees encroach   and nights are dark—

but not for now   not the wolf
but guns for sure   bombs, gas,

land mines, all kinds—

I watch you now   like a movie,
at your door   the guileless entry

You can't hear me shout
There's someone in the house

Yamma Comments on Literature

When the summer fields are mown /When the birds are fledged and flown,
I remember copying in cursive, leisurely sweep of joined letters,
words nicely spaced, work of a human hand.

From Longfellow's "Aftermath," about old age and the rowen,
summer's second cutting, not to be confused with Rowan,
a tree with red berries and lately a stylish name.

What to young Rowans do the names of trees mean,
the qualities of meadow grass,
or the clip-clop of sturdy verse?

Seasonal successions are gone, even the time
to sigh about them.Who sighs any more and whose life
paces still through stately, well-timed diminishment?

Accuracy

When I told him about the buffalo
left dead on the plains, the killing of buffalo
so that there would be no more Indians
about the carcasses left to beasts and weather
bones piled so high you could walk and not touch ground
and about the haulers selling bones to burn
for refining sugar or to carve into buttons
all about the wasteful cunning of it
the bones sticking in my throat as I spoke
he asked *Bison or buffalo?*
his mind a granite impossible
to inscribe, an impervious surface,
one of those new graffiti-proof train cars
gliding steely on its track

Sugar

Beginning At the East River . . .

where Cuban ships sat low in the water
with the weight of the stuff

DOMINO
upward slanting signature

yellow bag of the purveyor
anonymous master

"dedicated to sweetening the lives of countless"
fish perhaps gathered to savor what stevedores lost

A Kind of Honey . . .

When crystalized, easy
to sell. You get your land,

you get your cane,
get your people

trade in a triangle,
neat visual—

from Africa, go west,
make molasses, take it north,

and sail rum back, a map
of orderly industry

sugaring over
the devil himself

Nice . . .

You must surround yourself with nice things
she said, my mother at coffee,

center of the table, metallic bouquet,
a vase of silver spoons

I chose one to stir, then propped
it for her to polish when she washed up

One spoon ribbed like a scallop shell
wide as a smile, rugged to the lips,

was for scooping only
(a wet spoon leaves lumps in sugar)

Even Now . . .

what I most often want
is the long ago, withheld

then proffered, dangled
to be earned or to keep me still,

sweet that meets no need, appetite
cheaply appeased,

my craving fed from snowy chutes,
arrangement seeming absolute—

At the river, a police boat speeds by, chin up.

Expendable

Who's not?
Including the young,
                    blanketed in cement
or in silent bundles
pressed to bloody chests.

Hard to say what separates us
from those lying down,
                    reasons for our current safety
known, if at all, to God alone,

who's left us "Thy Will Be Done"
and headed for the hills again,
                    after claiming that even the worst of us
belongs in this dance of particular parts.

From Zion Shall Come Forth Instruction.

(Isaiah 2:3)

End Times as usual, fierce debates, a stench shrouds the podiums,
how can they breathe, yet they talk on and on,

Moloch is back for the little ones

Surely this, the long promised Apocalypse

How could people

Cries from a lower floor, a baby's up, someone is coming, this
place is safe

Elsewhere the mothers look asleep, beside stilled bodies, their
children wait

How could people where is

Shekhinah

mobile beyond all motion

God's effusion, Wisdom?

Yamma Looks Up from the News to Wonder

It seems to me we've been getting along
along some edge or limit
of somebody's patience
and we've been testing it.

After he freed the beasts from the ship,
what did Noah do but barbecue,
(smoke of burning flesh smearing air
never again so fresh),

and this clumsy way of thanks
or apology moved God to guarantee
clemency, an inconsistency
leaving a margin, a DMZ,

where life persists
via grace or negligence.

Yamma Witnesses June 12, 2020

When there was still talk of keeping track, Leigh and I took a walk to see what was up, to witness the story, to record for a safer day what it was like on Broadway.

We saw plate-glassed banks boarded up, no more pretense of transparency, restaurants too sealed tight, plywood against the citizenry, blank fronts belying something lost, in sheen or substance, of amity and trust.

We stopped at the obelisk on 25th to read that General Worth *was led by love of nation,* high sentiment expressed in bronzed Latin.

The *polis* was an abandoned stage set, monuments intact, but not the politics—citizens in masks, begging cups tied to sticks.

Yamma on Charity

Your hand, he said as if
to himself. *Your hand
is soft.* I took this
as a compliment.

Yes, I thought, my hands
are nice, he was right
to admire them.

Gloving for dishes
or small garden labors,
plying them at night
with sweet lotion,
I would remember
the coins I gave him
with satisfaction.

Sestina on 6th Street

It's good that they are there
When we need to be good—
The ever-present poor
Watching out for us,
For a moment
When we wake up.

When we wake up,
We want to be good.
We say, "Look at the poor
By the burning barrel there!
What would it cost us
To be with them for a moment?"

Or on the street, the moment
The man asking for money looks up,
We wonder, "What is he doing there?
What makes him not like us?
Will we become as poor
If we are not good?"

The poor know how to be good
At being poor.
They know how to fade from us
Times we are not up
To their sadness. In happy moments,
They spare us, they won't be there.

They have a way of being there
When we need someone poor
To take our old clothes, still good,
To say “God Bless” to us,
And for a moment,
We think their prayer raises up.

Their mercy rises up,
The reckless mercy that in a moment
Accepts the gift in spite of us,
Takes indifference for good,
Finds love that is not there,
The mercy of the poor.

Sad as rain, the poor,
And as munificent, and there
Always, the poor always with us.

Yamma Considers Herself as an Ancestor

I scheme to strike a pose
to leave to you, though who knows

which worst moment may lodge
in your memory, or word I never meant.

Worse yet, how can I represent
those already absent, my stories

stripped of their vision or intent, tales
strung from incidents, documents

that are scarcely legible,
hear-tell, bills of sale—

August 6

Let me tell you a story of the bomb
that brought your great grandfather home.
That bomb was the start of me and later you
(so this is your story too). It was enough
to start the plot, the knot
where the skein of my story starts,
this scheme of loops drawn from a tangle.

                                        There was light unspeakable
illuminating nothing that I want to tell you—

I've told you about your great grandfather arriving home
because they dropped (you must understand) the bomb—
and how to crochet, how to mind the pattern, yarn loose
but under control—that skill could be my legacy,
along with this tale.

A Joyful Mind Maketh Age Flourishing

Proverbs 17:22

Let Go

In the clarification of moonlight,
I felt myself just a creature, no need
to manage, improve, or explain.
I was just another being in time,
and since any name—so saints have said—
is poverty, no sense despising what I am.

And hadn't the sunset's vermillion
felt like confirmation?
As if I, though no
great specimen—not straight
nor full nor tall—could still
leaf out and let go.

Retired

I thought I
was made to
be moving
about, about
something or
other, but
instructions
couldn't be clearer:

staying useless
makes me less
of a bother.

Not One Leaf Has Left That Oak

It's like me with all my teeth,
still on two feet, waiting
for the bus as I watch
the tree now brown in death—
yet in spring coming back
as if dying were a joke

          and maybe it is, I'm not
willing to bet, but let the question
rest, allowing momentary shifts
to suffice—

          sun to ice, dark to light,
from cold to the bus
and the warmth of us

Yamma Practices Yoga

Half slumbering, no thought but breathing,
rising belly all that is moving,
my tired bones a heap, concrete, each part
still as cinderblock, ash compressed
from burning, no fire in what is left.

But still my soul in air incoming,
the density of myself pervading,
so that what was tough enough
for withstanding is suddenly soft,
bright and living, new colors
in the bleached coral bed
filling spaces left for dead.

Nap

Hands about a book,
I nod and trek
in snow to something
sudden and intact,
a deer's ribs,
unsheathed canoe,
elaborate snow shoe,
curved struts half sunk,
cave that held
heart guts lungs not
unlike my own.

Nature's a ghost
weighed down
in bones
I rise to write
but put aside
to watch the woods
turn white.

Last Summer

The white roots of the easy-go
jewel weed were fine as hair, thin
as the tendrils of my attention,
which kept reverting to float and distance,
abstract by default, above it all
as I swam up and down the lake,
fishes' lives beneath my notice
along with bird calls, shifting clouds,
and the one wild flower
that sowed itself to a purple mound
on scarce sun behind the barn.

One night, Helen remarked upon the moon
as we drove home. Undeterred
by talk, she kept looking, leaning back.

Yamma Considers Taking a Trip

Why go, since I'll drag along
the same thrum thrum?

Better to stay still,
watch clouds and seasons roll,

observe one branch leaf or swell,
backyard birds take up their calls.

I'm a body encasing
a metronome,

no escaping
its tick—my only medium.

Sun comes soon, soon gone.
June scald of high noon.

From me, no encomiums,
but hiss—*not this, not this*

must be something else—
Why go anywhere since

I march to that dull drum,
not seeing what I look upon?

Light Between the Trees

spills, indiscriminate.
                                        Each trunk
takes the touch, blessing of warmth
in a bright path downhill to the brook.

Why is my plaint always my wrongness
and need to accommodate, my one joke
myself, inadequate, immune
to mercy?

            In a quiet town among
traffic lights' civility, banking hours,
donating to the library, a harmless lady.

Yamma at the Christmas Light Show

That gaudy time of year again,
when I'm brought here to watch
the stricken trees decked out in lights.

Someone's purled purple bulbs in rows
along trunks that spout chartreuse
and rainbows lead to the silent carousel.

A night out for the old girl, they think,
but I bet the whole lot can't wait
for the scene to evaporate and me

brought back to bed in assisted care,
no lipstick, what's left of hair
every which way, just me, tucked

and curled up, insubstantial bulk
beneath starched sheets, little me,
this weasel, so much regrettable,

soul to be ceded back to the general.

Untitled

What you just said?
Name of a face?

A new phase.
Is there a phrase

for this phase?
I was once

made of phrases.
I had to construct

little pauses
to hold them back,

my mind a library
with a—what is the term?

something with cards,
a cabinet, cards, orderly

something there used to be
in a library—

A Dull, Sublunary Poem

Personally, I have never been attracted to the moon,
an afterthought, chip off the old block, ravaged face
spotlit as if to make us look

(*Look at the moon!* someone
will always say to you, as if it were
something new.)
                                        But what's worse,

mornings like this, there it is,
suspended above Motor Vehicles,
imposing its chilly presence

over those of us seeking license
to be on our way, insecure
while the moon moons along on its

sinecure, slowly growing dim,
a fragment not even a planet
set on shining on this place
                                        without me in it.

Yamma Considers the Counterfactual

Relating to what is not the case:
serving to warn, as in,

Do that and God knows
how things will turn out.

Doubt was our baggage
in matters of marriage and mortgage.

It was a jungle out there, teeming with ifs,
pitted with traps for heedless steps.

That there could also be
rare birds perched, counterfactually

magnificent, makes me regret
our vigilance.

Anniversary Celebration

In a predictable release, each unremarkable leaf
consigns itself to sidewalk slush
through which we lurch, inevitable pair
to treat ourselves to dinner, where
we will marvel that we've lasted so much
longer than anticipated
and concur that change is overrated.

Life provides such narrow choices:
Subatomically, it's lepton or quark;
at all levels, alternatives are stark—
though a cell assigned the heart might voice
desire to join the leg's design, it must
take its nature as a sign.
Look at twins separated at birth
who discover when they meet again
they've both married women named Elaine.

Who says variety is worth the strain?

Yamma Writes a Letter

I saw the tree you called your own,
its bark dented with a wooden ladder,
now almost gone. But it couldn't hold you
anyway, daughter like me,
apt to crave your privacy.

If you were here today—

                                        yet asking that asks
too much—

                                        The pond brims
and at its edge, another year of violets.

Core

As old ice is an archive, a stack of tales told in ash, pattern awaiting discovery, my life too might reward your scrutiny, layered as it is with events untold and contrary. My mind at this time is a subduction zone, drought-blasted ground where seismic changes once took place, but I bet that underneath, you'd find glazed melt lines that tell of times unaccountably sweet.

Blood Root

I’m slimming down
and packing up
my thin store
of what’s what

No more
knowledge
in general,
I’m sticking to
the ephemeral.

Particularly,
to that one
white bell
that swells
swaddled
so tenderly.

Yamma Attends Services as Usual

In the time it takes the boy
to fetch the book

and the time it takes
the priest to open it

and then the time for him
to speak, we wait.

He is an old man.

In the time when
little is left for me

to say or see,
I may begrudge

with the fading of the pulse
the time I've spent here,

but where else?

The Good Book

It’s about words,
a bravura performance
of sounds promising substance—
praises and supplications,
secrets and directions,
words kind and unkind
heaped and irresistible
until they swamp the mind,
don’ts and dos and doubts
devolving to sound and fury—

Or it’s all about
the plot—a heart
looking for its story.

Yamma's Vocabulary Is Hopelessly Dated

Now that   previous manifestos
and ideas about   what to expect next
are moot   and suspect,

I can offer only   word collections,
hazy observations,   or (forgetting Mother's caution)
just trying to get attention,

and all I have   to say to you   sounds
laughable   I an old girl   "skinny and adorable"
vocabulary   "so 20th century."

But there has been   from time to time
a sound   or a touch   a hum or a brush
a breeze   a hand like light rain

a weight lifted   all at once   a home
and destiny—   If I could   leave you
those moments of—   was it certainty?

Yamma Contemplates the Final Scene

The hospital bed, daughters arriving,
flowers, everyone busy,
me not complaining,

set on remaining pleasant,
a cheerful old lady
brave, complaisant,

though allowing in conversation
a few hints of suffering
kept from observation.

Perhaps a priest, oil on the brow
full circle from the first time,
which I missed somehow,

infant me busy self-assembling,
not ready to buy into
what I was seeing.

Until that scene, the wheeling
galaxies are not pausing
for me self-medicating

with episodes of *Nature,*
soothing myself in full color
with tenderness for leopard and spider.

Yamma Would Like to Sum It All Up

You'd think, on the brink
myself of one, I would
come to some kind
of conclusion

Yamma Contemplates the Way

Well, I've gone quite a way, haven't I,
gone *a good long way,* as they say, at my age.

It's a question of which way, I suppose,
with scanty maps, no compass rose.

Maybe the Way was the joy in transit—in the car,
with you, a loving interlude to who remembers where,

or alone along the loop my habit carved uphill,
back to the burning bush that flamed each fall,

or in a tunnel when train windows darkened,
and we apprehended—suddenly—ourselves illumined.

All I can say is, I've gone many ways,
as many as a tree ramifies in branching,

or a river at its mouth sheds itself,
all force and elaboration subsuming seaward.

Notes

"Yamma After the Ferry Ride"
Italics from Walt Whitman, "Crossing Brooklyn Ferry"

"Alimentary"
Italics from Blaise Pascal, "Man is only a reed, the weakest in nature, but he is a thinking reed. "

"Worms"
. . . contributing to the world's grain harvest as much as Russia
"Worms produce as much grain as Russia, researchers say"
—*The Guardian* September 29, 2023

This is how we sing as the species' ship goes down Elizabeth Willis "And What My Species Did"

Ruin from the air.
—Gordon Thomas and Max Morgan Wits *Ruin from the Air: The Enola Gray's Atomic Mission in Hiroshima*

"Yamma Reads Iris Murdoch's Definition of Humility"
"In *The Sovereignty of Good* (1970), Iris Murdoch came up with one of the best, most economical definitions of humility, which is simply 'selfless respect for reality'."
—Costaca Bradatan

"Final Act"
What's done cannot be undone. knocking at the gate.
—*Macbeth* Act V scene i

"Sugar"
". . . Domino® Sugar has been dedicated to sweetening the lives of countless bakers . . ."
—itsallpink.com

"A Kind of Honey found in cane, white as gum, that crunches between the teeth."
—Pliny the Elder

". . . with devotion's visage, we sugar o'er the devil himself. "
—*Hamlet* Act III scene i

"Expendable"
"For Wisdom is mobile beyond all motion, and she penetrates and pervades all things by reason of her purity."
—Wisdom 7:24

About the Author

Elizabeth Poreba—aka Yamma to her three grandchildren—is a retired New York City High School English teacher, now reasonably busy as a foot soldier for climate causes. She spends most of her time in New Lebanon, NY with John Poreba, her husband of more than five decades.

Her work has appeared from time to time in *Commonweal.* She has published two collections of poems, *Vexed* and *Self Help* (Wipf and Stock, 2015 and 2017), and two chapbooks, *The Family Calling* and *New Lebanon* (Finishing Line Press, 2011 and 2023). Her work is also in *This Full Green Hour,* an anthology composed of work by six of the O'Clock Poets (Sonopo Press, 2008).

Find out more about Elizabeth at:
elizabethporeba.com

www.ingramcontent.com/pod-product-compliance
Lightning Source LLC
LaVergne TN
LVHW051020080826
845145LV00009B/2710

* 9 7 8 1 6 3 9 8 0 6 0 8 9 *